The Dopamine Guide: How to Naturally Improve Your Focus, Motivation, and Mood by Stewart Wright

Copyright © 2024 Stewart Wright

All rights reserved. No portion of this book may be reproduced in any form without permission from the publisher, except as permitted by U.S. copyright law.

The Dopamine Guide: How to Naturally Improve Your Focus, Motivation, and Mood

By

Stewart Wright

Chapter 1

When dopamine levels in the brain are low, it may lead to a number of negative outcomes, including a lack of motivation, fatigue, addiction, mood swings, and memory loss. Together, we will discover how to increase your dopamine levels in a natural way.

When it comes to motivation, productivity, and attention, dopamine is an essential neurotransmitter that plays a significant influence in all of these areas.

Dopamine is a neurotransmitter that plays a role in the overall feeling of well-being that you experience.

The decisions you make in your lifestyle, the food you eat, illness, and a great number of other variables may all contribute to decreased dopamine levels, which can leave you feeling exhausted and uninterested.

In the event that this describes you, it is possible that your symptoms are the result of a low dopamine level.

What is Dopamine?

Approximately 86 billion neural connections may be found in the normal human brain. Their ability to communicate with one another is made possible by neurotransmitters.

One of the neurotransmitters that has been the subject of the most extensive investigation is dopamine. This is due to the fact that it is associated with a wide variety of aspects of human behavior, such as feeling motivated, seeking pleasure, and developing addictions. Dopamine is present in high concentrations across the animal kingdom, and it is probable that our even larger quantities are a part of what differentiates humans from other animals. It plays a role in a range of processes, including attention, memory, mood, learning, as well as movement, anticipating pleasure, and learning.

It contributes to our high level of intelligence and assists us in developing complex social connections, making use of language, planning, and setting goals for ourselves, as well as for our family and friends.

The dysfunction of dopamine is the underlying cause of a few illnesses, the most known of which being Parkinson's disease, which is brought on by the death of cells that produce dopamine. Others include Alzheimer's disease and schizophrenia.

Dopamine is produced by a few number of neurons, and those neurons that do create it are concentrated in a few particular regions of the brain. These regions include the amygdala, which is frequently referred to as the "fear center," and the hippocampus, which is also known as "the memory center of the brain."

Dopamine is essential to the functioning of several systems that are not part of the central nervous system. These systems include the kidneys, the pancreas, and the cells that make up the immune system.

Due to the fact that this dopamine is made locally, it is limited in its ability to easily pass across the protective blood-brain barrier that exists inside the brain.

Dopamine’s Structure and Function

It is common practice to categorize neurotransmitters according to their function, which may be either excitatory or inhibitory.

When there are inhibitory neurotransmitters present, the chance of a nerve impulse firing is reduced. On the other hand, when excitatory neurotransmitters are present, the likelihood of an excitatory neurotransmitter firing significantly increases.

In terms of its chemical composition, it is categorized as a monoamine, which puts it in the same category as serotonin, which is another neurotransmitter that plays an important role in the regulation of one's mood.

How Does Dopamine Affect Us?

Following our discussion of the fundamentals of dopamine, let's move on to the ways in which it influences our day-to-day lives.

The neurotransmitter dopamine is sometimes referred to as the "motivation molecule." It is responsible for enhancing your motivation, concentration, and attention. It enables you to plan ahead and resist desires, which ultimately enables you to achieve the goals you have set for yourself. After you finish the work at hand, you will experience a sense of achievement. It will stimulate your competitive tendencies and offer the thrill of the chase in many aspects of life, including business, sports, and love. It will give you the sensation of "I did it!" after you have completed the task.

Furthermore, dopamine oversees the pleasure-reward system in your body. It enables you to experience sensations of pleasure, contentment, and even euphoria. When you have insufficient dopamine, you may become inattentive, uninspired, sluggish, and even sad. Dopamine is so important for motivation that lab mice that are lacking in dopamine are unable to motivate themselves to eat. They will opt to starve even if food is readily accessible if they do not have enough dopamine.

It is often difficult to maintain a lifestyle that includes all of the necessary nutrients in order to maintain optimal brain health and function. What exactly is the reason for this? Stress, poor food choices, lack of sleep, medications, pollution, and other factors are all nutrient thieves, which means that they rob the brain of the nutrients it needs in order to function properly.

Chapter 2

It is possible that taking nutritional supplements might contribute to the following:

- promotes restorative sleep, which is essential for the brain to get in order to regenerate and repair itself
- assists you in developing a greater resistance to stress and assists in preventing mental tiredness
- supplies the brain with the food it need in order to produce the highest possible level of mental performance

The Signs and Symptoms of a Lack of Dopamine

If your dopamine levels are low, you will not have any enthusiasm for the environment around you. The lack of energy and drive will compel you to rely on stimulants such as coffee, sugar, and other substances to get you through the day. This is a frequent symptom of the flu.

Listed below is a list of the symptoms that are most often associated with a lack of dopamine:

- apathy
- behaviors that are harmful to oneself, such addictions in particular
- weary state
- an absence of hope
- The inability to successfully complete duties
- a lack of ability to concentrate one's attention
- having a tough time developing meaningful ties with other individuals
- an inability to feel pleasure in whatever form it may take
- a lack of drive to do things
- a deficiency in sexual desire
- problems with one's memory
- changeable moods
- procrastination of tasks
- a lack of sleep

Dopamine deficiency has been linked to a wide range of mental illnesses, including but not limited to depression, attention-deficit hyperactivity disorder (ADHD), schizophrenia, Parkinson's disease, Alzheimer's disease, and addictions of all kinds.

Causes of Low Dopamine

Dopamine deficiency may be brought on by a wide range of various situations and circumstances.

Insufficiency in Nutrition

It is possible that a lack of l-tyrosine, an amino acid that is a precursor to the creation of dopamine, might be the consequence of a diet that contains an insufficient amount of protein altogether.

Another possibility is that you are lacking in one or more of the cofactors that are necessary for the transformation of l-tyrosine into dopamine. These cofactors include, but are not limited to, vitamin B6, vitamin B9, copper, zinc, or iron.

The Supplements That Are Not Correct

Certain natural supplements have the effect of lowering dopamine levels, thus you should steer clear of them if your goal is to raise dopamine levels. These supplements include:

- 5-HTP
- licorice root powder
- The bark of the magnolia tree, also known as Magnolia officinalis
- melatonin
- Neoni fruit, also known as Moringa citrifolia
- mulberry, sometimes known as Morus alba

Chapter 3

High Histamine Levels

Dopamine levels are decreased when there is a high concentration of histamine. Therefore, regulating histamine helps to optimize dopamine levels. The following are some methods that may be used to reduce histamine.

What is Histamine?

The histamine receptors that histamine binds to determine the effect that it has. Scientists have discovered four different types of histamine receptors; however, we are only going to discuss one type because it is the one that is concerned with sleep. Histamine is responsible for a number of functions in the body and plays a significant role in the body's response to inflammation.

H1 Receptor

You contain H1 receptors in every part of your body, including neurons (brain cells), smooth muscle cells in your airways, and blood vessels. When the H1 receptors are activated, symptoms of anaphylaxis and allergic reactions appear. This may result in the following:

- Itchy skin, also known as pruritus
- Vasodilation, also known as the expansion of blood vessels
- Hypertension, often known as low blood pressure
- An elevated heart rate, also known as tachycardia
- Flushing
- A narrowing of your airway, also known as bronchoconstriction
- Aching
- Permeability of blood vessels, which refers to the movement of fluids via cells in blood vessels
- Rhinorrhea, often known as sneezing, stuffy nose, and runny nose

Not only do H1 receptors keep allergic responses under control, but they also aid with the following:

- Patterns of sleep and wakefulness
- Consumption of food
- Temperature of the body
- Feelings and emotions
- Recalling
- Instructing

Because drowsiness is a common side effect of certain anti-allergy medications that block histamine signaling, histamine is considered to be a wake-promoting neurotransmitter. Additionally, histamine neurons are generally active in wake states and inactive during sleep. Histamine neurons promote wakefulness by activating neurons in the cortex that cause arousal and by inhibiting neurons that promote sleep. In other words, histamine ensures that you remain awake.

Foods that Reduce Histamine Include:

- Apples
- Onion
- Pineapple juice
- Parsley
- Blueberries
- Olive Oil

Because vitamin C also has the ability to lower histamine levels, every meal that contains vitamin C has the potential to lower histamine!

Avoid the following foods if you are attempting to lower your histamine levels:

- Kombucha
- Alcohol
- Meats or cheese that have been aged
- Olives
- Apple Cider Vinegar
- Tomatoes
- Avocado;
- Onion greens

Histamine-lowering supplements that may be helpful include:

- The supplement forskolin
- The antioxidant quercetin
- vitamin C
- The probiotic strain known as B. longum and a strain of the probiotic bacteria B. infantis
- Pancreatic enzymes (see a physician before doing so)
- Methylxanthines (Dietary sources of methylxanthines include coffee, tea, chocolate, maté, and guarana. You can drink coffee, eat chocolate, or supplement with theobromine, but attempting to supplement with theophylline is not recommended, as adverse cardiac effects are possible. However, chocolate also contains some histamine, and researchers suspect that it may encourage histamine release. The net effect of cocoa is unknown; it's recommended that you test your own individual response and see what it does for you.)
- The fisetin
- Luteolin, which may be found in broccoli, parsley, and celery and
- EGCG, which may be found in green tea

• Kaempferol, which may be found in products such as grapefruit, witch hazel, cruciferous vegetables, and delphinium plants

• Myricetin, which may be found in a huge variety of vegetables, teas, wines, and berries

• Rutin, which may be found in passionflower, apples, and buckwheat

• Theanine, which may be found in both black and green tea

• The reishi mushroom's

• Eleuthero, which is often referred to as Siberian ginseng

• Tulsi, which is sometimes referred to as holy basil

• Mucuna pruriens, which is also often referred to as velvet bean

• Lactobacillus plantarum, which is a probiotic

• Palmitoylethanolamide, often known as PEA

• Valerie, which may be contained in foods such as meat, cereals, vegetables, milk, and other dairy products

Insufficient levels of dopamine have been linked to a wide variety of health problems, including the following in particular:

- Depression
- Obesity
- Addiction

There is a whole category of prescription drugs that are referred to as dopamine antagonists. These drugs work by binding to dopamine receptors in the brain, which in turn inhibits the effect of dopamine.

Drugs that fall within this category may be broken down into three basic categories: tricyclic antidepressants, drugs that treat nausea and vomiting, and certain antipsychotic medications.

Alcohol, marijuana, cocaine, methamphetamine, ecstasy, amphetamines, and LSD are all examples of recreational chemicals that have the ability to alter the circuits that are responsible for the processing of dopamine, resulting in a dopamine roller coaster.

Caffeine, sugar, recreational drugs, shopping, video games, cell phone use, online porn, gambling, the pursuit of power, and thrill-seeking are all examples of behaviors and substances that have the potential to be addictive.

These substances and behaviors flood the brain with abnormally high levels of dopamine, which causes the brain to become addicted to the substance or behavior in question.

If you want to increase your dopamine levels in a natural way, you don't have to resort to engaging in activities such as "sex, drugs, and rock 'n' roll." Instead, there are a number of approaches that are safe and have been proven by scientific research.

Poverty, loss, domestic abuse, and social discrimination are just a few instances of terrible hardships that should be taken into consideration. Extreme difficulty may have a detrimental influence on dopamine production over an extended period of time.

It is also possible that a chronic influence of a traumatic childhood event, such as being mistreated or growing up in the household of an addict, might be the cause of low dopamine production.

EMR is an abbreviation for Electromagnetic Radiation. One of the most surprising sources of dopamine depletion may be your smartphone. There is evidence that the electromagnetic radiation released by mobile phones, along with serotonin and norepinephrine, affects dopamine levels, which is a dual-purpose stress hormone and neurotransmitter that aids in the response to stressful events.

Chapter 4

For dopamine to increase, one of the following must be true:

- There is an increase in the production of dopamine
- The rate at which dopamine is being broken down is decreasing.
- A greater amount of dopamine is being recirculated throughout the physical body
- The numbers of dopamine receptors that are being produced are increasing.
- Dopamine receptors that are already present are operating at a higher level of efficiency

The term "raising dopamine" is used throughout this book as a simple shorthand for the whole spectrum of alterations that are being discussed. This term refers to the total collection of neurochemical changes.

Unhealthy behaviors have the potential to lead to an increase in dopamine levels. Dopamine is created whenever you participate in an activity that is essential for your existence, such as eating, drinking, having sex, or earning money, for example. This strategy ensures that you continue to do what you need to do in order to survive (in contrast to the lab mice that were deprived of dopamine, which were discussed before).

It is possible for natural activities to increase dopamine levels by fifty to one hundred percent in comparison to baseline levels. On the other hand, pharmaceuticals have the ability to increase dopamine levels by millions of times higher than natural activities.

A small percentage of people who engage in potentially addictive and self-destructive behaviors are aware that they are "self-medicating" in order to achieve a dopamine rush. These behaviors include smoking cigarettes, which increases the production of dopamine by 200 percent, cocaine by 400 percent, and amphetamines by an incredible 1,000 percent.

Dopamine stimulants, which include things like caffeinated drinks and sugary meals, tobacco products that include nicotine, and prescription prescriptions, as well as activities like shopping, sex, video games, online porn, power, and gambling, may lead to major issues in your life if you use or abuse them.

Here are eleven natural ways to increase dopamine in a way that is healthy.

1. Healthy Diet

Apples, avocados, bananas, beans, eggplants, oranges, peas, and plantains, along with spinach and tomatoes, are some of the foods that have been discovered as containing high amounts of the neurotransmitter dopamine. This is despite the fact that there has been very little research conducted to establish which foods contain dopamine.

Dopamine that is consumed via food, on the other hand, does not cross the blood-brain barrier. If you want to enhance your dopamine levels by eating, you will need to discover a method to get around this barrier through some means.

The amino acid l-tyrosine, from which dopamine is formed, is often found in high-protein foods like meat and chicken. Consuming a diet that is abundant in l-tyrosine will ensure that you have the essential building blocks that are required for the formation of dopamine in your brain and circulation.

Below is a list of foods and spices that are known to contain l-tyrosine or to promote dopamine production via other ways. These foods and spices are listed chronologically:

- products extracted from animals, including meat, poultry, fish, eggs, and dairy products
- apples
- avocados
- bananas
- acorns
- olive oil
- oregano
- peanuts
- turmeric (cumin)
- some watermelon
- raspberry

Fava beans, also known as broad beans, are one of the few foods that contain l-dopa, an amino acid that is a direct precursor to the neurotransmitter dopamine. Fava beans are also known as broad beans. This is due to the fact that l-dopa is able to pass through the protective blood-brain barrier. L-dopa is the current gold standard therapy for Parkinson's disease.

Natural probiotic foods such as yogurt, kefir, and raw sauerkraut, among others, may help to improve the body's natural dopamine production. Surprise, surprise: 50 percent of the dopamine in your body is in your intestines, where it is generated by bacteria in your stomach. It has been discovered that the Bacillus, Escherichia, and Serratia genera, as well as the species Lactobacillus plantarum, may produce dopamine in the human stomach, according to available data. The quality of your gut flora has an influence on the amount of dopamine your body produces. There can be an overgrowth of harmful bacteria produces toxic byproducts known as lipopolysaccharides, which have the potential to kill cells that produce dopamine in the brain.

Some Beverages That Stimulate the Synthesis of Dopamine

Caffeine is the beverage of choice for millions of people all over the world to begin their day. Caffeine helps you feel more awake and alert because it stimulates the release of dopamine and increases the availability of dopamine receptors in your brain. Coffee, tea, or any other caffeinated beverage is the product of choice for these individuals.

However, caffeine is not the only substance that has been shown to increase dopamine levels. In teas of all kinds, including black, white, oolong, and green contain an amino acid, l-theanine. Unlike caffeine, l-theanine is known to promote a feeling of relaxation in the body. It easily passes the blood-brain barrier, causing a rise in dopamine, serotonin, and GABA levels in the brain, which is a neurotransmitter associated with calm. L-theanine is also available by itself as a dietary supplement.

2. Stay away from foods that deplete dopamine in your body.

If you want to increase your dopamine levels, you should avoid certain meals. It has been shown that increasing your intake of saturated fat, which can be found in animal fat and palm oil, will reduce the sensitivity of your dopamine receptors.

Sugar consumption has been shown to increase dopamine levels; however, this increase is only temporary and unhealthy; it is more similar to the effects of drugs than it is to those of food, and it eventually leads to a shortage of dopamine. Additionally, you should avoid using artificial sweeteners as a substitute because it has been demonstrated that aspartame reduces the levels of dopamine and serotonin in the brain.

Enhancing Supplements for Dopamine

In the conventional sense, there is no such thing as a dopamine pill; however, there are a variety of natural supplements that are available that work in a variety of ways to raise dopamine levels in the brain. Some of these supplements increase the actual quantity of dopamine that is available, while others prevent dopamine from being broken down too quickly. Other supplements either increase the number of dopamine receptors in the brain or assist the receptors that are already present in the brain in functioning more effectively.

It is recommended that you have a look at the following list of some of the best supplements for naturally enhancing dopamine production:

L-Tyrosine

L-tyrosine is the first dopamine supplement that should be looked at further. This amino acid is a precursor to the neurotransmitter dopamine. Tyrosine is actively transported across the blood-brain barrier, where it is eventually converted into dopamine, which is then released. It is impossible to generate enough levels of dopamine if you do not get enough l-tyrosine in your diet or if your body does not correctly convert it. It is possible that you may need more l-tyrosine if you are under stress, exhausted, or suffering from disease.

The fact that tyrosine is especially helpful in boosting tolerance to extreme stress is yet another benefit of this amino acid.

Mucuna Pruriens, also known as Mucuna Pruellens

Mucuna pruriens is a tropical legume that contains l-dopa, which is a precursor to the neurotransmitter dopamine. Mucuna supplements are offered to boost general brain health as well as anti-aging and libido. In addition to improving mood and memory, mucuna pills are also sold to enhance libido and anti-aging.

In the treatment of Parkinson's disease, which is characterized by low levels of dopamine, it has been discovered that this herb is even more effective than levodopa medications. Mucuna supplements should not be used by individuals who have Parkinson's disease. Before using any mucuna supplements, you should consult your physician.

Turmeric (Curcumin)

Turmeric contains the active ingredient curcumin, which is the primary active ingredient. It easily crosses the blood-brain barrier, resulting in an increase in dopamine levels in the brain. Curcumin has been proven to be just as good in treating depression as the widely used antidepressant Prozac. To maximize absorption of curcumin, look for a curcumin supplement that also contains piperine, a compound found in black pepper that increases curcumin absorption by an astounding 2,000 percent.

Ginkgo Biloba

Ginkgo Biloba is a kind of plant that grows throughout Asia. Ginkgo biloba has been used to treat circulatory problems, asthma, vertigo, fatigue, tinnitus, and a variety of brain-related problems such as poor concentration, memory problems, headaches, mental confusion, depression, and anxiety for more than 1,000 years. Ginkgo biloba is a plant that is native to China and has been used to treat a variety of ailments for more than 1,000 years.

One way to do this is by enhancing the transmission of dopamine in the prefrontal cortex, which is the part of the brain that is accountable for language, thinking, decision-making, and planning.

SAM-e, bacopa, arctic root, ginseng, kava, citicoline, phosphatidylserine, and resveratrol are some of the other supplements that have been proven to increase dopamine levels. Other supplements that have been linked to this effect include resveratrol.

The Essential Nutrients That Are Needed

In conclusion, the production of dopamine in the body requires a number of critical components, including vitamins, minerals, and essential fatty acids, among other things.

You should make sure that you are getting sufficient amounts of the following nutrients, either via the food you eat or through the supplements you give yourself:

- The B vitamins, including B6, B9, and B12
- vitamin D
- Magnesium
- Iron
- Omega-3 fatty acids

Exercise

It has been demonstrated that engaging in physical activity can increase the formation of new brain cells, reduce the aging of existing brain cells, and improve the flow of nutrients to the brain. Additionally, it has the potential to raise your levels of dopamine, serotonin, and norepinephrine. Physical activity is one of the most beneficial things you can do for your mental health.

Ratey, MD, a notable psychiatrist and author of Spark: The Revolutionary New Science of Exercise and the Brain, has undertaken a substantial amount of study on the impact that physical exercise has on the brain. Ratey has researched the effects of physical exercise in a broad range of contexts.

He made the discovery that engaging in physical exercise raises baseline levels of dopamine by promoting the formation of new receptors. Dopamine, in combination with endorphins, which are naturally occurring painkillers, is responsible for the experience that is often referred to as "runner's high."

On the other hand, you do not have to engage in strenuous physical activity in order to reap the benefits of this kind of activity for your brain. In fact, it is possible that doing so will be detrimental. For example, researchers found that thirty minutes of running on a treadmill did not result in an increase in dopamine, whereas one hour of yoga did result in an increase. Walks and gentle, low-impact exercises like yoga, tai chi, and qigong, as well as meditation, can all provide significant mind-body benefits. Even something as simple as getting up and moving around more frequently throughout the day can help to counteract the effects of prolonged sitting, which are known to deplete dopamine levels.

The quantity of dopamine receptors in the brain increases as a result of exposure to sunshine, which also creates vitamin D, which activates the genes that release dopamine. If you are able to do your workout outside, this is an even better option.

Meditation

Approximately one thousand research papers have been undertaken on the subject of meditation and its benefits. Meditation has been shown to create a healthier and more robust brain via a number of processes, including the following:

• ensures that the body's neurotransmitters, including dopamine, remain in a state of equilibrium

• improves the functional capacity of synapses in the brain

• lessens the amount of inflammation in the brain

improves the brain's ability to adapt to new situations

• increases the volume of blood that is coming into contact with the brain

- decreases the synthesis of hormones that deal with stress

One piece of research has shown that regular meditation practice has the potential to increase levels of dopamine by as much as sixty-five percent for certain people.

Listening to Music

Dopamine is produced when we listen to music that we like, and the pleasure center of your brain becomes active whether you are making music, listening to music, or performing music.

It is not even necessary to listen to music in order for this neurotransmitter to be released; even the anticipation of listening to music can accomplish this. Have you ever listened to a piece of music that causes you to feel warm and fuzzy on the inside? This sensation is associated with a significant increase in dopamine levels.

Socializing

Dopamine is released in response to all types of pleasant touch. A therapeutic massage increases dopamine production by 31 percent while simultaneously decreasing production of the stress hormone, cortisol, by an equal amount. Hugging triggers a release of neurotransmitters that are beneficial to the brain, such as dopamine, serotonin, and oxytocin (also known as the "love hormone"). Petting your dog may provide a rush of dopamine and a plethora of other feel-good brain chemicals to both you and your pet.

It has been established that tickling or having sexual contact may increase dopamine levels in experimental animals; however, this has not yet been demonstrated in human subjects at this time.

Despite the fact that it is not always feasible to get a massage or to offer a hug, it has been shown that merely participating in pleasant social interactions with other people may enhance dopamine levels without the necessity for physical touch.

Chapter 5

Getting enough sleep is one of the most important things you can do to maintain and improve the health and performance of your brain. Dopamine appears to play a more important role in sleep regulation than previously thought. It regulates the synthesis of the hormone melatonin, which is responsible for sleep. Lack of sleep may result in a reduction in the number of dopamine receptors in the brain. Even one night of sleep deprivation resulted in the downregulation of dopamine receptors.

First, the quantity of sleep that one should get is different for different people of different ages. If you want to figure out how much sleep you need, you need to think about your overall health, the things you do every day, and how you typically sleep. Here are some things to consider that may have an impact on your individual needs. It is essential to understand that these are general recommendations. You are an individual, and as an individual, your needs may be different from those of other people.

Here are some things to consider that may have an impact on your individual needs:

- Do you sleep for seven hours and wake up feeling healthy, joyful, and active? Or have you discovered that you need more sleep in order to get going in the morning?
- Have you been diagnosed with more than one health condition that may need you to take extra time off?
- Are you someone who expends a significant amount of energy on a daily basis? Do you participate in sports or have a profession that needs a lot of physical labor?
- Do you often engage in activities that demand you to be attentive in order to carry them out in a secure manner? Do you drive a lot on a daily basis or operate large pieces of machinery? Do any of these activities ever cause you to feel sleepy?
- Are you now experiencing difficulty sleeping, or have you ever had difficulties sleeping in the past?
- Does caffeine make it easier for you to get through the day?

- When you have a lot of spare time, do you have a tendency to sleep in a little bit later?

Depending on how you respond to these questions, you will be able to determine the amount of sleep that you need.

Oversleeping

Individual concerns are important, but there is a limit. The majority of people are aware that getting too little sleep can be detrimental to your health. Sleeping too little on a consistent basis is linked to a number of chronic diseases, in addition to making you irritable and tired during the day. However, did you know that sleeping too much can also be detrimental? Oversleeping is linked to a number of health problems, including the following:

- Type 2 Diabetes
- Heart Disease
- Obesity
- Depression
- Headaches and migraines

Is it possible that sleeping too much might make you ill, or is it an indication that you already have a problem? In any case, if you find yourself falling asleep or longing for the next nap, you should probably schedule an appointment with your primary care physician.

The fact that you need more than eight or nine hours of sleep each night in order to feel calm may be an indication of a more serious issue. There are a number of factors that may impair the quality of your sleep, causing you to feel exhausted and lethargic even after spending eight hours in bed. Other factors include the following:

- Sleep apnea
- restless legs syndrome
- Bruxism, often known as teeth grinding
- A persistent ache
- Prescription medication

If you have checked out those issues and you are still hitting the snooze button after nine hours of sleeping under the covers, it may be an indication that you have a heart problem, diabetes, or depression. If this is the case, you should consult a physician. The physician may also recommend a sleep study to ensure that there are no sleep problems.

Lack of Sleep

Sleep deprivation is a term that refers to the situation in which an individual does not obtain sufficient amounts of sleep. However, there is a more comprehensive notion known as "sleep deficiency," which incorporates sleep deprivation in addition to other problems. Sleep deficiency may be caused by any of the following:

- Lack of sleep
- Sleeping at the wrong time of day
- Low quality sleep

People need to sleep just as much as they need to eat, drink, and breathe, and it is just as important to your health and happiness as these other things. According to the Centers for Disease Control and Prevention, approximately one-third of people in the United States do not get enough rest or sleep every day. Additionally, nearly forty percent of people say that they fall asleep during the day at least once a month when they didn't intend to. Additionally, between fifty and seventy million Americans have sleep problems that don't go away. Sleep deprivation can lead to issues with your physical and mental health, accidents, decreased work output, and even an increased risk of death. Sleep deprivation can make it difficult to perform well at your job, school, driving, and with other people. You may find it difficult to learn, pay attention, and move around. Additionally, it may be difficult to

It is possible for children and adults to exhibit various symptoms of sleep deprivation. For example, children who are not receiving enough sleep may exhibit behaviors such as being extremely active and having difficulty paying attention. Additionally, they may engage in misbehavior, which may negatively impact their academic performance.

Adults, teens, and kids who don't get enough sleep are also more likely to get hurt. For example, sleepiness while driving is a major cause of serious injuries and deaths in car accidents. When it comes to older people, not getting enough sleep may make them more likely to fall and break a bone. People who don't get enough sleep have also made mistakes that led to terrible accidents like nuclear plant meltdowns, big ships running aground, and plane crashes.

People often have the misconception that they can get by with less sleep and that nothing negative will occur. However, studies have shown that having sufficient amounts of quality sleep at the appropriate times is essential for maintaining mental and physical health, as well as quality of life and safety.

Chapter 6

Weight Loss

Dopamine dysfunction and obesity are closely related to one another. Obese people have a lower number of dopamine receptors than the general population, and their brains have a connection with food that is very similar to that of a drug addict. Because dopamine is in charge of the pleasure center of the brain, individuals who are overweight experience less pleasure and satisfaction from eating, which encourages them to consume more food.

It is recommended that you give intermittent fasting some thought if you are having difficulty losing weight. This scheduled approach to eating may help in the maintenance of the health of dopamine receptors, in addition to assisting in weight reduction.

You have undoubtedly heard a lot of crazy weight loss advice over the years, such as replacing meals with "cookies" or drinking celery juice every day. These tips are frequently promoted by people who aren't very knowledgeable about health, so if it sounds too good to be true, it probably is. However, for those who are in the right mental health space and have weight loss as a personal goal, there are plenty of valid, research-backed, and expert-approved recommendations out there as well as a ton of misguided weight loss advice that should be avoided.

There is a lot of research on the benefits of plant-based diets. The results of a study that involved over 200 dieters showed that those who followed a plant-based, low-fat diet for 16 weeks lost significantly more weight than the control group. The study was published in October 2022 in the journal Obesity Science & Practice. One of the suggestions that has been made is to make changes to one's diet. The findings of a study that was published in February 2023 in Nutrición Hospitalaria revealed that researchers examined data from over 15,000 individuals and found that those who consumed the fewest processed foods had a lower risk of obesity, while those who consumed the most processed foods had an elevated risk.

An online support group can help boost motivation, according to research that was published in Digital Health in July 2022. Another study that was published in June 2022 in the Review of Communication Research came to the conclusion that social support is associated with better adherence to weight loss behaviors. This conclusion was based on a 10-year review of literature on the topic of social support in online obesity health communities. Numerous studies have also indicated that having strong social support—whether it be from friends, family, a coach, or even an app or online community—can be beneficial when attempting to lose weight.

When you are attempting to lose weight, you need also take into consideration your attitude. According to study that was published in the journal Obesity in February 2022, persons who successfully lost weight accepted their failures and considered them as momentary pauses in their strategy rather than as indications that they had failed.

Eat Slowly

In addition to boosting our pleasure of food, eating slowly enhances our capacity to detect when we are full. This is because we do not always notice when we are full.

Take the Time to Savor Your Food

We're often told what to eat, so when we don't enjoy a particular food, we're less likely to form enduring healthy eating habits. Give new fruits and veggies a try. Learn how to make new, flavorful dishes that offer variety. Spices and herbs can enhance the flavor. Alternatively, relish the richness of raw and steamed vegetables and the sweetness of fruit. It's not impossible to have a happy relationship with food.

Maintain a Daily Gratitude Journal

Whether we are aware of it or not, there are instances when our eating habits and our emotions are related. We might turn to food as a coping mechanism when we're stressed. I help clients practice gratitude by having them write in a journal on a daily basis, or even just when they're feeling stressed. This way, when stress arises, they can recognize it and find other ways to deal with it instead of turning to food as a coping mechanism.

Prepare and cook in Large Quantities

I might, for instance, prepare a large quantity of chicken on Sundays so that it would be plenty for the whole week.

Lifting Weights

Make sure that you lift weights at least twice or three times per week. Increasing your muscle mass can be accomplished by using weights that range from moderate to heavy. This can be accomplished by performing three or four sets of ten to fifteen repetitions with weights that are difficult for you. When you have more muscle in your body, it is more likely that food will be used as fuel rather than being stored as fat.

Get Enough Sleep

Lack of sleep can lead to weight gain because it raises the hunger hormone ghrelin and lowers the satisfaction hormone leptin. We crave more sweet and salty foods when we don't get enough sleep. For what reason? Because your cravings for foods higher in energy, or calories, intensify whenever you experience greater hunger. Inadequate sleep is also known to impact our ability to think clearly and manage our emotions, so it's not difficult to draw the connection between this and a reduced capacity to make rational decisions in a variety of life domains, including eating. If we were to flip the coin, we could reasonably conclude that our bodies function better when we are well-rested. That would imply that we would only eat until we were fully satisfied when it came to eating. Because our bod

Don't Skip Meals

Keep in mind that staying alive is our bodies' primary objective. Our bodies literally need calories for life, so as soon as they are denied to us, they will take action to survive. Foods with a higher energy density are recognized by our bodies, and we will crave them more. Let your body know when it is hungry, but don't let it believe it is starving. This contradicts a lot of diet strategies, but those strategies don't really benefit people in the long run. Generally speaking, I advise eating every four hours.

Try to Stay Hydrated

According to studies, those who drank two glasses of water before meals lost more weight than those who did not, and they were able to keep the weight off. This simple piece of advice serves two purposes: first, anger may be mistaken with hunger, which can lead to overindulging in food. Secondly, drinking water while you are eating makes you feel fuller.

Reduce Calories

By selecting options such as strong cheddar rather than mild cheddar, you may reduce the amount of cheese you use while still preserving its taste without making you feel as like you are on a diet.

Organize Your Plate

When you rearrange the portions of vegetables and grains on your plate, you will notice a difference. When you do this, potatoes, corn, and peas belong in the grains category because they are starchy vegetables. Also, divide your plate in half for vegetables, and then divide it in quarters for whole grains and a quarter for lean protein.

Regardless of where you are, take things one step at a time. Refrain from feeling as though you must make drastic changes to your entire life right now. Determine your current situation and your desired future state after that. Purchasing a step counter and measuring your daily walking distance is an excellent place to start for individuals who lead mostly sedentary lives. Next, aim for a step goal that is marginally above average and gradually increase it to a daily target of 10,000 steps.

Think On the Big, Not the Little

You should pay attention to the "big rocks" of weight loss. There are a few areas in which you will get the best value for your money. Putting those first and letting go of everything small that adds up to stress will make achieving your goals seem easier and more manageable. When it comes to nutrition, you should be mindful of the amount of calories, protein, and fiber you consume. When it comes to exercise, you should prioritize recovery, daily steps, and strength training.

Look Beyond the Numbers on the Scale

Although it is helpful, the scale is not the only factor to take into consideration. It is a good idea to keep a running list of victories that do not involve the scale, and to take regular measurements and photographs to assist you in evaluating progress that may not be reflected on the scale. This will help you maintain perspective and highlight all of the positive changes you are making to your overall way of life and health.

For breakfast, try to get 15 to 25 grams of protein. Protein helps you feel full because it slows down the breakdown process and reduces hunger hormones. A high-protein breakfast also helps prevent cravings from occurring later in the day. Try eating high-protein frozen waffles with nuts, berries, and a touch of maple syrup, or two eggs with whole-wheat toast and avocado. Pair protein foods with fiber and healthy fats.

Consume Protein With Each and Every Meal

Protein has a beneficial effect on your hunger hormones and slows down the digestive process. Additionally, protein can fend off hunger more effectively than carbohydrates. Some examples of foods that are high in protein include quinoa, edamame, beans, seeds, nuts, eggs, yogurt, cheese, tofu, lentil pasta, chicken, fish, and meat. Consuming foods that are high in protein at each meal, especially breakfast, can help the individual lose excess weight.

Try to eat foods that are mostly whole and just sometimes processed. When people are given unlimited access to ultra-processed foods, research indicates that they may consume up to 500 more calories per day than they would if they were given unprocessed foods. This is because processed foods have a significant amount of added sugar, fat, and salt. Additionally, the numerous processing stages that are involved in the production of processed foods cause them to taste so good and make us want more.

Try to cut down on the amount of high-glycemic sweets you consume. How quickly blood sugar rises after consuming a carbohydrate-rich meal is measured by the glycemic index. When high-glycemic carbohydrate foods like white bread and potatoes are consumed, especially when they are consumed alone, blood sugar levels will rise and then quickly fall. You become hungry and want more food as a result of this. While more extensive research is required, preliminary findings indicate a connection. However, high-glycemic foods are not completely forbidden. Working with a registered dietitian-nutritionist can offer customized strategies to help you balance your diet and avoid blood sugar spikes, which can help reduce appetite.

Desserts may be made using a variety of fruits. Fruits are high in nutrients, such as fiber and antioxidants, and low in calories. Just 10% of Americans are getting enough fruits and vegetables, according to the Centers for Disease Control and Prevention. In addition to helping you fulfill your daily needs, having fruits for dessert will enhance the flavor of your meal. A lot of fruits work well baked, grilled, or sauteed. For instance, grilled peaches with shaved almonds and vanilla yogurt on top are delicious!

Generally speaking, you should consume more calories in the morning. According to research that was published in the journal Nutrients in November 2019, participants who were given small breakfasts and large dinners lost a significantly smaller amount of weight than those who were given the opposite schedule. Thus, it is possible that eating smaller meals later in the day will benefit people who wish to reduce weight and enhance their general health. The study's intriguing finding was the timing of dinner consumption. They discovered that eating the larger meal, or main course, after 3 p.m. was linked to difficulties with weight loss. It's crucial to understand that this study does not advocate for a 3 p.m. mealtime for everyone. Individual needs—such as those who are pregnant, nursing, have diabetes, or take medication that requires specific foods—may necessitate the need for extra snacks and food. It is crucial that you consult with a registered dietitian or nutritionist for this reason.

Plan Meals

Taking five to ten minutes on the weekend to plan your menu for the upcoming week will save you time, money, and unnecessary calories in the long run. If you are having trouble deciding what to have for supper tonight, don't worry about it because it is already on your menu plan. Creating a menu helps you stay organized, keeps track of the groceries you need to buy and the ones you already have, and ensures that your plate is balanced. It is important to remember that taking a night off from cooking and preparing a frozen meal or ordering takeout is perfectly acceptable. The benefit is that you will know in advance that you will be doing that, which prevents you from having to scramble for food when hunger strikes. Additionally, it is important to put the plan in writing; this will serve as a constant reminder and increase the likelihood that you will adhere to it.

Creating and Adhering to a Shopping List

As soon as you have your weekly menu planned, you should make a shopping list, either on paper or on your phone (I use Notes, but there are apps for this as well). Having a list of the things you need to buy at the grocery store will help you avoid wasting food, save time, and avoid buying things that just happen to look good but are unnecessary. If you want to stick to your list, you should avoid shopping when you are exhausted or hungry. Studies indicate that there is an increase in impetuous behavior during those times.

Investigate Each and Every Item in Your Kitchen

You need to have the right supplies and kitchenware on hand in order to prepare nutritious meals. Low-sodium canned beans, canned fish, tomato sauce, whole-grain pasta, quinoa, brown rice, low-sodium stock, low-fat plain yogurt, an assortment of fresh and frozen fruit and vegetables, olive oil, and dried herbs and spices are some basic items I suggest keeping in your pantry, refrigerator, and freezer. These are just a few of the components that can serve as the foundation for a tasty and healthful meal.

Have the Necessary Equipment

Similarly, easy, effective, and healthy cooking can be ensured by stocking your kitchen with a variety of useful tools. For instance, I love using a seasoned cast-iron skillet for cooking eggs, sautéing vegetables, and making pancakes because it reduces the amount of oil or butter, I need to use to prevent food from sticking. An immersion blender, an Instant Pot, baking sheets, measuring cups, spoons, and a hand juicer are a few more of my favorite kitchen tools. Of course, having a good set of knives is a must for anyone working in the kitchen.

Investigate the Labels on Food Products

It is important to note that calorie content matters when trying to lose weight in a healthy way, so it is important to read labels carefully. Making it a habit to open your packages on the other side can help you save money, time, and even calories. Food labels provide you with an accurate picture of what you are actually consuming. To ensure that you are getting a balance of nutrients in your diet without consuming excessive amounts of sugar, salt, or saturated fat, you should make sure that you are reading labels carefully.

Snacks

It's best to consider your snacks to be little meals. Since we are snacking more than ever, it is best to select healthful snacks, such as Greek yogurt with fruit on top or almond butter with sliced apples or high-fiber cereal. Nutritious snacks can help bridge the gap in your diet and increase feelings of fullness and satisfaction because it can be difficult to get everything you need in one sitting.

Chapter 7

Cold Showers

Taking a long, cool shower can increase dopamine. If you're not up for that, at the very least conclude your shower with a spray of ice water. Taking a shower with water that is 14°C/57°F can significantly increase dopamine levels, by as much as 250 percent. Cold shower proponents claim that taking a cold shower improves their mood and productivity throughout the day, even more so than drinking coffee. Cold showers also lower histamine, which may contribute to the increase in dopamine.

Learn to Take Advantage of Your Brain's Reward System

To survive, dopamine triggers the release of energy when a fantastic opportunity presents itself. When our needs are met, dopamine is released into our system. We enjoy dopamine surges because of the pleasant sensations they provide. But the relentless chase for your next dopamine spike may transform you into a "wolf on Wall Street," driven by addictions, greed, and lust. Here are two healthy strategies to adjust your dopamine level that work with your brain's built-in reward system to enhance, rather than damage, your life.

Pleasure in the Quest

Our remote ancestors were involved in a continual quest merely to live. They experienced a dopamine boost every time they noticed a fresh cluster of berries or a better fishing area, since this meant survival. While you may not still harvest berries and fish, there are many healthy ways you can enjoy the quest of living a contemporary life. Find new music to download, unique materials to cook with, a budget trip package, a hard-to-find collector's item, or the ideal present for a loved one while foraging on eBay. Geocaching, genealogy, bird watching, and collecting of all types are all examples of quest-oriented hobbies that you might pursue.

For the reason that there is always something new to discover in these kinds of activities, they are good for sustaining dopamine levels in the brain. The release of dopamine is enhanced with each new discovery that is made.

On a daily basis, you should do the "Victory Dance." It is likely that you have seen football players pounding the ball on the ground and doing a celebration dance after scoring a touchdown. The euphoria of victory is great, and this is due to the fact that it causes a surge of dopamine to be produced.

Unfortunately, such “touchdown moments” don’t come frequently in regular life. But you may purposefully promote dopamine release by pushing yourself with new objectives. A little amount of dopamine is produced every time you complete a goal, no matter how big or small. Break down your big goal, such as "getting organized," into a series of smaller goals to achieve it. It is possible to achieve each goal in a straightforward manner, such as organizing your emails, cleaning a closet, or emptying your junk drawer. Every time you complete one of the tasks on your to-do list, you should experience a small rush of dopamine.

In an ideal scenario, your objective should be challenging because the more challenging your goal is, the more sense of success you will have, which will result in an increase in the amount of dopamine that is produced.

Recognize and enjoy your accomplishments on a regular basis in order to get a daily boost of dopamine. Additionally, when you have accomplished a particularly significant goal, you should perform your own version of the victory dance!

Final Thoughts

The "motivation molecule" dopamine is in charge of your pleasure-reward system. Enough dopamine ensures that you will feel more alive, focused, productive, and motivated throughout the day. There are both healthy and unhealthy methods of increasing dopamine production. Self-destructive behaviors and addictions can result because of unhealthy ways of thinking. Eating the right foods, engaging in physical activity, meditating, and employing effective goal-setting techniques are all examples of healthy ways to increase dopamine.

References

Alban, P. (2021, August 2). *How to increase dopamine naturally (comprehensive guide).* Be Brain Fit. Retrieved April 18, 2022, from https://bebrainfit.com/increase-dopamine/

Dopamine: What it is, Function & Symptoms. Cleveland Clinic. (n.d.). Retrieved June 11, 2022, from https://my.clevelandclinic.org/health/articles/22581-dopamine#:~:text=Dopamine%20is%20a%20neurotransmitter%20made,%2C%20mood%2C%20attention%20and%20more.

Cristol, H. (n.d.). *Dopamine: What it is & what it does.* WebMD. Retrieved June 11, 2022, from https://www.webmd.com/mental-health/what-is-dopamine

Watson, S. (2021, July 20). *Dopamine: The pathway to pleasure.* Harvard Health. Retrieved June 11, 2022, from https://www.health.harvard.edu/mind-and-mood/dopamine-the-pathway-to-pleasure

Hochwald, L. (2023, April 7). *Lose Weight the Healthy Way with 25 Tips From Registered Dietitians*. EverydayHealth.com. https://www.everydayhealth.com/diet-and-nutrition/diet/tips-weight-loss-actually-work/

Histamine. Cleveland Clinic. (n.d.). Retrieved April 19, 2023, from https://my.clevelandclinic.org/health/articles/24854-histamine

A;, B. A. K. R. K. P.-L. (n.d.). *Learning and memory*. Handbook of clinical neurology. Retrieved April 19, 2023, from https://pubmed.ncbi.nlm.nih.gov/24112934/

Anti-histamine foods. Root Functional Medicine. (2023, January 5). Retrieved April 19, 2023, from https://rootfunctionalmedicine.com/anti-histamine-foods

Foster, J. (2021, September 9). *9 natural antihistamines used to prevent histamine reactions*. SelfDecode Supplements. Retrieved April 19, 2023, from https://supplements.selfdecode.com/blog/natural-antihistamines/

Therapeutic Goods Administration (TGA). (2022, September 27). *First-generation oral sedating antihistamines - do not use in children*. Therapeutic Goods Administration (TGA). Retrieved April 19, 2023, from https://www.tga.gov.au/news/safety-updates/first-generation-oral-sedating-antihistamines-do-not-use-children

;Watson NF;Badr MS;Belenky G;Bliwise DL;Buxton OM;Buysse D;Dinges DF;Gangwisch J;Grandner MA;Kushida C;Malhotra RK;Martin JL;Patel SR;Quan SF;Tasali E; ;Twery M;Croft JB;Maher E; ;Barrett JA;Thomas SM;Heald JL; (n.d.). *Recommended amount of sleep for a healthy adult: A joint consensus statement of the American Academy of Sleep Medicine and Sleep Research Society*. Journal of clinical sleep medicine : JCSM : official publication of the American Academy of Sleep Medicine. Retrieved April 18, 2023, from https://pubmed.ncbi.nlm.nih.gov/25979105/

Paruthi S;Brooks LJ;D'Ambrosio C;Hall WA;Kotagal S;Lloyd RM;Malow BA;Maski K;Nichols C;Quan SF;Rosen CL;Troester MM;Wise MS; (n.d.).

Consensus statement of the American Academy of Sleep Medicine on the recommended amount of sleep for Healthy Children: Methodology and discussion. Journal of clinical sleep medicine : JCSM : official publication of the American Academy of Sleep Medicine. Retrieved April 18, 2023, from https://pubmed.ncbi.nlm.nih.gov/27707447/

Oversleeping: Bad for your health? Oversleeping: Bad for Your Health? | Johns Hopkins Medicine. (2021, October 20). Retrieved April 18, 2023, from https://www.hopkinsmedicine.org/health/wellness-and-prevention/oversleeping-bad-for-your-health

U.S. Department of Health and Human Services. (n.d.). *What are sleep deprivation and deficiency?* National Heart Lung and Blood Institute. Retrieved April 18, 2023, from https://www.nhlbi.nih.gov/health/sleep-deprivation#:~:text=Sleep%20deficiency%20is%20linked%20to,adults%2C%20teens%2C%20and%20children.

Made in United States
Troutdale, OR
12/22/2024